“A Mourning Dove’s Wishbone”

A Book of Poems

by Megan Denese Mealor

ISBN: 978-93-95224-01-7

First Edition: 2022
Rs. 200/-

Cyberwit.net
HIG 45 Kaushambi Kunj, Kalindipuram
Allahabad - 211011 (U.P.) India
http://www.cyberwit.net
Tel: +(91) 9415091004
E-mail: info@cyberwit.net

In loving memory
of Erma and Gene Mealor,
Mammaw and Pappaw,
my rock and my shoulder,
now reunited with my beloved father,
their long-missed son.

"Poetry is an echo,

asking a shadow to dance."

-Carl Sandburg

Contents

Dude Ranch Dues

We corresponded cowpuncher chaquetas
dogging each other on savanna Steeldusts
indefinable amid furrowed bluebonnets
longhorns clashing limestone looms
the talismanic Texas half-light minting
live springs hutting hounded doves

Fitful cedar fences, uncoupled chuckwagons
harvested gangrenous hacienda hutches
forging beetled bygone byres
silhouettes of rough-stock rodeos
raddled Rio Grande steer-roping roots
harnessed hills humming with dragonheads

Mexican Hats waged war on white-tails
Prairie-Fire wrangled coast pipe corrals
Cowpen Daisies scandalized severed soil
Brown-Eyed Susans haunted railroad residue
Crow-Poison colonized fluted waysides
Garden Rockets seduced a limoncello sky

Upon Turning Thirty

I abandoned you in Apalachicola
sipping firewood fumes
and culling your camouflage
back where obliging framed porches
are oiled with shrimpers and shorebirds
ducks are cleaved from tupelo trees
Dead Man's Fingers flood old lace sands
one cloistered laser lemon light orbits
a soggy settlement of riverfront freewheels
ghost crabs galloping for drastic grooves
bleached featheredged fences akimbo

Absquatulate

backseat buttercups
decrypt the speedway sinew
of precursor ploughboys
reeking of nerve-ray
and shrewd Suwanee dogma

fiberoptic fairgrounds
parrot pirates, echo with ignition
detonating sky bows
latticework spiderlings
glassed line origami autobahn

laurelled libraries
grumble with skittish sophomores
linchettos, limnology, Lorelei
caesuras, buried Koine, shopiltees
spunky physics of black swan queens

rattlebrained roads
croon with cyanide Julias
gaslight rabbiteye
linchpin of lablab ladders
cardiac map of cornerstones

narcotized navies
bombinate bathing orchids
besiege bowheads and dottybacks
poaching mulloway pendants
hijacked hymnals of bottled half-seas

Decibel

I read your leaves in the unfiltered sake bar
by the rhetorical retail park on Lois Lane.

You left the *rihaku* and the *renkon* to me,
tackling a crash course of black sulfur ramen,

acidulated soybeans, three pikes of cartilage,
grandfathered fin flippers jarring my compass,

sputtering brass tacks about the blazing of
Yoshiwara's moated cathouse, how only just

three years ago, it was crooked to footloose
at Tokyo twilight. We rationed coffee jelly

while I driveled about seven thousand islands,
a hundred vibratile volcanoes, heaving brooklets

of haiku. The cherry-merry waitress with the
oxblood devilock rigged an asymmetric bill

ballooned with anomalies and wasp cookies,
your graceless demand for stilted didactics

and my handsewn habit of hedging all bets
before enigmatic horses can blow sky high.

The Blind Pig Live

bashment of bindlestiffs
Argus-eyeing a pending
beach volleyball barn burner
hoddy-noddy highballers
repressing Cape Codders
gingered Moscow Mules

a callipygian tapstress
garnishes Glencairns
deluding dipsomaniacs
chasing her conceit
with roughhewn ponies
coprolalia ovations
distilled devoirs

napkin doodles of beefy Impalas
rummage sale Civil War tintypes
neon bronco rider needlepoint
scalloped ropework overmantles
arranged in baroque blossoms
littering mustard sycamore brick

carved fruit maple carpet rockers
button tufted nailhead divans
rolling arms and tri-toned verges
floral-finished washstand fossils
tiled serpentine backsplash
bracket-footed, rouged

Dogtrot

When I was an ear-splitting eight,
we dwelt in the ruins of a belated dogtrot
that reeked of rose wine and blistered acrylic carpets,
its embossed wallpaper shedding
Maiden Pinks, bonesets, blue Japanese roses.

Gabled ironstone chimneys
sputtered spruce and blackthorn,
corralled cherry stairwell
leading up to flyblown lofts.

Circumscribed front and rear porches
secured sheds steeped in hickory handles,
moisture meters, citrus-honed chisels.

The pine-shingled rooftop
hosted a molded copper eagle
that elapsed and evolved
in the bobbish downslope.

A liberal corridor lined the family equator,
divorcing my father's horseshoe kitchen
from my mother's tiger oak secretary,
his earshot from her eyeline—

ever those iambic intervals between them.

Photo Album

kingfisher daisies
line our welded memories
bloom of potted sky

Safari Blossoms

subtle cyan steel
grasps at gazania petals
coffers taking flight

Neptune Beach

fan palm fir A-frames
recline on black sand beaches
world of winged joists

Sea Ledge

an arrow crab molts
disinterring violet claws
brittle stars barrage

Driving By an Oklahoma Wedding

We clashed through the campestral quilt
of Slaughterville, contention heating our kernels
as we passed a wedding powered by Mary Laura and Merlot,
outland sunflowers flooding its hobnailed bones.

The hand-beaded bride wore spangled white smoke boots,
an orchid-laced chignon, all mint peach, demure damask,
her trembling father clutching his baneful sobriety.

A perpetual stampede of pansy-purple bridesmaids
sported burlap bouquets and cocky sways,
accompanied by a funereal procession of army buddies,
obsolete frat boys preening like fluorescent flamingoes.

The groom stood at studied attention,
pacing his palsied poise, every kicking pulse
of the South Canadian River kindling in
his coal-burned wandering eye.

Royal Botanical Gardens, Sydney

Laced into the shallow bay of Farm Cove
the governor's hand-loomed garden
boasts of Cadigal bones,
a pollen-penned canvas
seeping Weeping Lilies, sundials,
lingual fountains, filtered skylight fernery,
fungal frescoes of indigo.

We follow the Ribbonwood roots
through forks of flying-foxes,
imperiled hollows of Black Jezebels,
blue-banded bees shopping Purple Dazzlers,
billabong damselflies laying underwater lairs
as wolfish wasps electrify sickled comfrey.

Lanky lilies strut through lawless rockeries
as chamomile sunrays clasp prisms,
incurable banksias dignify shrublands,
butcherbirds impaling lacewings on rose thorns.

Easter

Another Easter spent
feasting on Jelly Bean Martinis,
sculpting butter lambs
with Nana's mastiff Escort
snoring by tabletop fire.

Aunt Bea smoked lemongrass,
shading wooden eggs
with Dappled Willow shrubs.

A whimsical Slovakian cousin suggested
we whip each other with willow rods,
sprinkle ice-choked water on the women,
then blacked out on the buffalo grass
after sneaking three Peeptinis,
two Blushing Scots, half a pitcher
of Nana's Tea Party Two-Punch.

Aunt Harley arrived in a felt foxglove bonnet
laced with tender golden ribbons,
not for a moment distracting from
those swollen, swindled lips.

Papa Bear worked the washy den
in a plush paisley bowtie
decoding poached pagan relics:
every fairy tale tradition
from Pancake Tuesdays
to Passion Plays,

straw doll Judas bonfires
to pitching pottery
off olive wood balconettes.

Cousin Kaylee supplied the wildwood rabbit salad,
hot-cross buns spangled with sunny raisins,
blossom bread drawn into dandelions.

Uncle Rio dispensed the Roasted Cacao bunnies
and flattened pennies from a Gator World pit stop,
raving on about the Timberwolves, the Raptors, the Jazz.

The triplets tore into jute-twined baskets
stuffed with chiffon peony barrettes,
Minnie Mouse compacts and combs,
microscopic, backstitched Bibles
beforehand highlighted, honed.

Prostrate

You skim a little Puce graffiti,
sip from a tumbler of lukewarm Darjeeling.

You mail a glistering chain letter
to your half-hearted half-sister in Chesapeake
because you know she will fail to pass it on
and you want *someone* to have evidence
of your very best efforts.

You listlessly pedal your cyclocross
through a levitating backdrop of loblolly pines
all the way to the red-light fringes
of your gutted hometown,
where Jane Doe junkies congregate
around lewd neon pick-up trucks,
tricking and tracking their next trance.

You pause at a moth-eaten chapel
dubbed Windsong Church,
catching wafts of gimcrack gospel
drifting in the unkempt daylight.

You wonder what your infidel mother
would say if she could see you imagining
this holy house's carved intestines:

a plexiglass pulpit presiding over
golden oak slatback pews,

heirloom hymnals hypnotizing
the spire sparrows,
painted glass apostles
depending, impending.

You have almost forgotten to exist
without her vivacious cinnamon hair,
her tangy trail of yellow diamonds.

You almost *did* exist
within the flowerless space
of that total eclipse.

But here you are now, self-righteous
in your cork bed flats and poured glass bib—
raw denim Sunday best—
littering the creek rock parking lot
with your prodigal noontime shadow,

still inconstant,
waiting to believe.

No-Tell

On the footsore motel TV screen,
lyrebirds reflect chainsaws
from a whitewash of tassel ferns,
claiming sanctuary in mine shafts
to wait out cancers of bushfire.

Her bones are soiled, unwashed:
a vivarium of lilac pin-up curls,
inkwell odes to the musical boys
she left behind in locker rooms
and on boiling Polish trains.

His echo is anchored, skin-deep,
resounding an ashless marcato,
cherry-bomb thunder on fossilstone.
He unchains his blue-eyed breakables
from the knotted arabesques.

She rations her shopworn relics,
from the crackle of her cardinal mouth
to nomadic blisters on garnished feet:
a rootless rosemary Ophelia,
spinning columbines from filiform.

The contused bedside console
whines beneath the wilting weight
of toasted breadline cigarillos
as songbirds simulate car alarms,
embezzling courtship canto.

A Bathing Beauty

Marvel Rea never stood a chance,
not against the goons in the garnet truck,
glassy gypsy oxfords clacking along
a murky sidewalk in pitiless echoes,
her sculptured sandy spiral curls
abstracting the sullen starlight
scattered along Compton Avenue
like shanghaied strawberry quartz.

Her French Language cologne
still cloisters the eucalyptus grove
where her dainty two-reel bones
performed their final curtsy
that orthochromatic waning.

Obsequies

It was a shammer reunion than I had forecasted
within the dripping brushstrokes of my illusions,
complete with caterwauls, cashmere clinging to clammy cotton,
the stale airport brimming with Gran's lacelike perfume.

And you with your honeybee-blonde curly lob,
puffy pink Chanel knock-off accordion handbag,
those Rule Breaker Red lips far too flamboyant
for your unsuspicious geometric façade:

how could I have unsung you showboating
my second-grade diary to Daddy,
sparkling like Cassiopeia
while he rammed the explicit entry
down my secular throat?

There were checkmates and back ranks then,
tutus beginning at the hip.
We composed bullet lists
on grasscloth walls
in UV ribbon ink.

This alligator-infested realm
where I have been solicited to load lamp boxes
with Mom's candela compilation of
goosenecks, boom arms, and torchieres
reprises its purgatory with a sea shanty strain,
polite plastic bones bouncing to the brackish music.

If Your Villain Returns

Yes, I took it all back, *yes*,
every last spiky, tearful treasure
I ever scrapped mall court money
in exchange for an atom of you:

an Air Force Blue Bible
laser-etched with my future initials
and a lopsided little buttercup,
dog-eared yet disinterested

the whittled wooden rocket ship
I tinted with acrylic nuances
in stains of sunless lime, seething red,
the most insolent of blues

an outer space-black bamboo scrapbook
rife with the unbleached rubble of me:
Eurotrash pageboy, Ophelia bralette,
dejected eyes peeping through deadlines

but like a cellar spider's crawlspace web,
classified sighs still rally and mourn,
harvested by the corn moon
prowling your shoeless condo

No Crystal Ball Needed

It's not fair when even psychics go unquiet,
bleating out lemons against the bookshelf rain.

This hellcat in stovepipe jeans with a migraine aura
supposedly has it in for me, often hunts me from
the treeless office park to my mint brick townhouse
sporting quartz countertops, ablaze with cartridge candles,
brandishing Rothko prints on all three lopsided stories.

Oh, and clocks—clocks have a peculiar signification
within the rock maple narrative of my entity:
exactly two lifetimes ago, a faulty banjo timepiece
was cast off on me by a substandard cousin.

I hammered it into her sculpted grave marker,
hacked the heads off family sacrifices of marigolds.
This dead cousin is vexed; she's the one who keeps
cloaking my car keys and smashing Chinese teapots.

That same life cycle, I was chartered to marry a wig maker
who colonized a toxic shop in Williamsburg.
He stank of lavender starch and painted ammonia,
his bluster inflated by fashionable deceptions.

Was I at least placated by this man?
Did he gift me clove sachets at Christmas?
Permit me unspoiled editions of Godey's Lady Book?

No, this watermark husband was feeble with trauma,
certain that his first wife, an undercover poet,
continued to dog our reeded marriage bed
well after her demise from dropsy, well after
I poached the ringleted phantasm's scrapbook perfumes
and edible violets, sidestepping the baronial alley
of church-bells and bricky girls in my barbaric quest
to butter upon bacon those half-rats in gambler hats.

I oil the psychic's agog fist with griping bills,
thank her for the sagas I inspired in her.
Whatever her crimes, she never failed to detect
the insecticide in my psychology.

Reparations

My out-of-date cousin surfaced twenty minutes late
to Grammy's eleventh-hour graveside service,
enrobed in off-the-shoulder bubblegum, ruffles on her biceps,
caustic aquatic notes scalding my whimpering eyes.
Her faux mink lashes were uncoordinated, thickset—
jumping spiders grasping hopeless prey.

She ankled up, barn-red comma heels drowning
in the showered Civil War cemetery grass,
chugging a coffin nail braided with marijuana
like she was depleting a Corpse Reviver #2
under the layer rays of a chichi Reno lounge.

Grammy's seed pearl rope convulsed against
that jutting collarbone, ruby halo ring detonating
her pink taffy bandbox manicure, rawboned wrist
overburdened with Bakelite bangles,
a sterling bookchain panel wristlet,
the copper leaf Bell Trading Post clamper
imparted to Grammy from my hangdog father
on her ninety-second anniversary
at the service-enriched housing high-rise
where her hummingbird-lit hobby loft
was congested with metallic flamingo balloons,
Black-Eyed Susans and Blue-Eyed Grass
in canary crystal vases camouflaging the chaos of stems.

My cousin, now perched like Lana Turner
in a church-rented back row metal chair,

never bothered materializing at that final bash,
although my aunt, her incurable mother, bribed her
to sign a pastel ice cream cones card stating
"You are the Mona Lisa in my life"
and taped it to a recycled cardboard gift bag
stifling floating Butterscotch Brulee candles
and a lacquered little handbook on origami.

I wonder now if Grammy can finally see through
my cousin's ostentation, if she still considers
my cousin the front runner, if she now regrets
that red-eyed Christmas when she gifted my cousin
a laser-cut dollhouse (picket fence, plywood chimney)
and me a reborn vinyl doll with a simulated heartbeat
that stopped functioning on the nine-hour junket home.

At Age Thirty-Seven

Thirty-seven years old and still no sign of
hotspot mountains. I am too repressed to pull off
leg kicks at weddings, even when my pushiest
nonbiological uncles plead. I am always stuck in
plum or periwinkle cupcake tulle, forever the
retrospect bridesmaid with the drunkest escort.

I am too obsolete to relearn high school Latin,
too dishonest to teach myself action origami.
I can no longer, in good conscience,
erode crochet underboob crop tops
scored from corporate hippie hawkers,
stockpile novelty unicorn keychains,
annex flapper dress fringe totes.

During which phase are you obliged to outlaw
your ham-fisted polychromatic braid flower,
commence donning formless soot-hued slacks and
those slashed-sleeve sheaths your aunt insists on
burdening you with at annual Christmas bashes?

I'll hawk mermaid cat cookie jars at yard sales,
stop exploiting dollar-store warm sugar vanilla,
actually start exerting those junk mail credit cards
for Nordstrom, Coldwater Creek, J. Crew,
learn to tolerate the tang of blood oranges,
to exude poignant daisies sown for the childless.

My age-old niece will deify these Rainbow Brite stickers,
will lionize the musty menagerie of My Little Ponies
still vamping nylon cotton candy mohawks.

The unfinished attic cages the militant board games
left unstirred by battle since that uncombed morning
you last framed the jazz apple kitchen's swing door,
just itching to confront the refrozen snowflakes
in your ghost-white soda ankle booties.
To my transient nephew,
I will transmit this scruffy Big Wheel
I used to patrol my pastel-painted precinct.

My mother may want Dad's iron basset hounds back,
but probably not. She'd hide them in a garage capsule
instead of flaunting them in her teal farmhouse cabinet.
Or else she would donate them to the nearest congregation,
regardless of byzantine Biblical interpretation.

Once upon an enameled time,
there was a resealable girl who preserved
a class project terrarium for five and a half years.
She flickered up and down balance beams,
wrote English papers for swanky girls in baby tees,
spritzed unsent letters in Lisa Frank keepsake boxes,
allowed her faint-hearted kid sister to monopolize
her tea rose velveteen Minnie Mouse platform bed
on vertical, vagabond autumn nights.

That arroyo of a girl has carried that bed on her back
all her life: across undersea mountains, through
black-tailed deserts obscuring towering vertical clouds.

Incoherence

It was *how* you overhung the spirit quartz rain
above Old Woman's Creek
that glibly thawed the syndromes
of my flickering convertible skin,
your fire-dancing into the furrows
of a heart gone breezeless.

Your upturned topaz scrutiny
detonated overdrawn overestimation,
the very counterfeit breath
when snow pellets dramatize ice crystals,
vampiric diamond dust needles
gnawing Sandusky supermoons.

With all the wiles of a Banded Tulip
spitting on tabbed sweethearts,
I candidly dog-eared the angular temper
of your truant longboard,
the impolite symmetry of mute swans
pluming such well-tailored contour.

Unpolishing Black Pearls

It is a sundance Sunday
and I am penning a poem—
well, trying to craft *any* ditty.
All I can unearth to evoke
is the euphoric screech of my son
as he unspools mid-air,
crashing back down on the
silent mini trampoline
with a nimble groove.

It's his spring break from school;
his reduced teacher crammed
Spring Mix Jelly Bellies
into his Sideshow Bob backpack
along with a bashful post-It
cramped with timid scribbling
letting me know that my son
may be the best and only reader
in that entire class of nine,
but he also refuses the potty
and can't comprehend silverware.

There was a chili-red A-B Honor Roll ribbon
taped to his spiral Goofy notepad,
so I considered the matter a wash
and rewarded my disorderly son
with a McDonald's plush tiki Stitch.

He cherished it for three exultant minutes
before suavely dumping his untasted
nuggets, French fries, and apple slices
into the overworked trashcan.

As I browse the grubby window,
a garish group of skeletal girls
donning lace-up ruffled eyelet
cruise by like emperor angelfish,
punctuating and escalating.
Their earrings are glued together
with neon-spirited feathers that
shiver in the tower slide breeze.

One of the femmes, glossy-browed,
a sable-skinned Lady Macbeth,
has embraced her dynamic hips
and lets her boyfriend jeans
downslide past her ass crack,
thong-less and howling.

Another gamine's corkscrews
stem gold metal alloy,
shameless at the roots,
more unreliable every daybreak.

They gang up around the sundown swings,
fists bundled in corset hoodie sleeves
as the chestnut leaves quarrel
about the politics of windstorms.

My son pushes his snoopy little face
beside mine, our Majorelle-eyed mirages
running wild in the unkempt window.
With a cherub's split-second fickleness,
my undone blonde son lifts his hopeful hand
to wave devoutly at the wannabe pin-up waifs
raining together at the swampy playground,
sassy and seraphic sunlight conscious
in his sinless sentiment.

My pecan pie son's nuclear carnival
tinges my every new poem,
its own retrograde circle of milk—
even the overcast pieces I carve around zodiac.

The jittery crop-top nymphs depart
to lazily rummage the boneless block
where shotgun houses are powered
with warm white snowflakes yearlong,
ruptured porches fawning with threadbare bucks
in French Crop hairdos, Pumas sporting fat laces,
off-the-peg hemp pendants exploiting
lemon sharks' forfeited fangs.

My son is boogieing to the beat
of a granular Iron Maiden video
in his markdown Odie socks,
swiping sips of my diluted Sprite
between ruffly, contemptuous solos.

This poem will be densely distorted,
will forget to underline aftermaths,
will decline to reinvent rainbows.

But right now, my son is pointing to
the mango pudding,
giggling and unbending.

I abstractedly persuade myself that the
cherry blossom sky is mobbed with pollen
and those weatherless maidens
were never, ever damsels, anyway.

Third Eye Sagas

The specters are starting to take over my reach-in closet,
already sardined with rusting halter tops, skittish stilettos.
These revenants exhale ashes of boat orchid funeral wreaths,
unbarred eyes hemic with beachheads and canyonsides.

The tinseled revivalist enslaved in a Bordeaux robe
dripping coquille feather sleeves arises every skyblush,
supplicating in Carpathian Romani at the cashew footboard,
offering up alms and psalms to any bleeding-heart angel,
a capsized Mary Magdalene exorcizing trumped-up demons.

Her crib-noting pepper shaker grandiose daughter
acute with Skylark foo foo, asymmetrical draped hip,
nourished by chiselers, alligator jazz, and torpedo juice,
robot-bombed this Fox Fields wedding cake-contoured
Second Empire baroque with cut stone, balustrades, and
Flagstone clapboard trim, gung-ho for a Governor's Palace
genuine fake manor on the hill, funded by her egg-beating
crab patch mother's pennies from heaven.

I don't have the heart to clarify hell-bent hydraulics
of astringent offspring to this forsaken lost sheep
primping dime store Art Deco hinged half hoops,
Bakelite bone, synthetic rock crystal asymmetry.
She warbles, an aweless wren, about her coterie of
polished Lucite poodles, penguins, toucans, leopards, bulls.

Neither can I summon the mettle to unfold to her
the quick-freezing fact that her peripheral overtures

are grasped only by a lonelily woman tardy on rent,
dreaming of circling sharks and headless folklore.

She implores me to recoup the gold architecture dangles
she was set in quartz stone about being laid to rest in,
rabidly insisting that her spitting cobra sister-in-law,
a mugbug Minnie Moocher who kicked the gong around,
navigating her wolfish wares from the brother's secretary desk
to his Louis XVI giltwood bed, hijacked the heirship earrings
before dramatizing her meteoric plunderage earned from
the groom's quick-tempered influenza mere weeks after
bartering his thriving uptown shoes sovereignty
for a thunderstruck sum.

The untarnished widow donned Gatsby ballroom crystal drops
at the cliff-hanging wake, the dead brother's loved ones
retreating in revulsion after paying final respects.

This roundheel sister-in-law never wanes from
the beggar banshee's tantrums for a peerless moment,
trapping her own figmental essence in slow-burn brimstone.
Her inexistence is panoramic.

A primitive, petulant lad in muddy pantaloons
boomerangs his lemon peel baseball up and down
the bronze-baked staircase on the declining occasions
our dethawing family receives visitors (mostly clammy priests),
his decomposing giggle waxing macabre hysterics
as our ruffled callers furnish their unmilled excuses,
making pyretic escapes.

My stepson has glimpsed this sunless kid pacing hallways,
swears to the very Lord that the insensible child's face
has depicted a vulture, a rat snake, a gurgling skull.

The unfinished war widow in the bias-cut gown with
a slashed backline, Red Cross Coquette air step heels,
black olive hair mantled in pin-up top victory rolls,
is by far the most unsaved and unforgiving of them all.

She crouches by the floral fireplace in the Surrealist den,
toiling to warm a gossamer pair of pipe dream hands.
I've withstood her frenzied dogma in the freshly-fussy
Amish-toned guestroom where she was reputedly throttled
on the parquetry parlor by her big-wheel lover,
an impeachable senator's son who never stood trial,
was wed within the year to the primrose niece
of the local Lutheran youth pastor.

The unseeing widow still huddles in vain
for her sweetie to return bearing yellow lilies,
cordial apologies, profound excuses,
the promise of poignance and children.
She doesn't miss her first husband, then or now,
a corporal who shattered on a gaping beach.

This piteous waif carved an unflinching eye
into the built-in butler pantry door,
frantic to imprint her shadowless survival.

Painting Party at an Indian Buffet

I am scumbling a cataract waterfall with underhanded oils,
ad-libbing the lilac current and dysmorphic October Glory maple trees.
Feeling prolific and pioneering, I fashion a festooned mermaid
headlining shamrock curls, gaudy beneath the lioness sun
atop an out-of-tune libertine boulder garden.

The pedestrian instructor clears her throat stormily,
downturned eyes resentful as solar streetlamps
behind her rimless blonde tortoise frames
as she earmarks my mutinous aesthetic.

My syndicated mother towed me to this loitering class
within a strip mall Indian dive, the peppercorn air pulsating
with bouquets of cardamom, mutton, unleavened flatbread.
The curry buffet winking with fairy lights is distended
with acerbic cuisine that begets my broken heart
to broil like a battery acid drip.

My mother's painting is, of course, timidly idealistic,
her sentimental waterfall poignant with larkish layers
of pewter, aqua, salmon, smoke, isabelline, silver bullet, bone.
Her tailored flapper bob is a last-word showstopper,
Cupid's bow lips nuanced as a silent starlet's enigma.

Her latest bank's silver manager extended the skittish invite
to what he broadcast as a "Paint and Sip Party with kebabs"
after Mom dropped by in a maroon leather pencil skirt
to dramatically deposit her fourth bona fide paycheck.

She keeps insisting (with no actual probing from me),
there is *nothing* amorous, schmaltzy, awkwardly sanguine,
or starry-eyed about his incidental entreaty.

Yet she took three-and-a-half hours to get dolled up,
discarding four-fifths of her smug diplomatic wardrobe
before culling the evergreen cable-knit sweater
Dad ponied up two Christmas Eves ago,
the most claustrophobic jeans in her swarming closet,
ultrasuede peep toe pumps and liquid eyeshadow,
counteracted by an Ethiopian emerald lavalier
vignetted against her unearthed collarbone,
Ferrari lips contradicting peaches-and-cream.

She must have pocketed a sunup manicure
because her embittered fingernails have been forged
into temporary silk periwinkle talons which clash
with her liberal yellow platinum coiffure.

I diagnose the sidekick savor of Chasing the Dragon Hypnotic,
sardined beside Mom at a reclusive folding crafts table
within the banquet room of two-month-old Curry Kingdom.
Diamond-studded notes of pink pepper and fir balsam mist her
marrow.
She must have wielded that crystal flagon wholeheartedly,
perhaps petrified of the sensual amber aura deserting her
along with her second, fifth, and eighth cherry pie cachets.

The rest of my slapdash classmates are barely propelling
their neophyte paintbrushes, far more stimulated by the
skyscraping stoneware plates stockpiled with butter chicken,
lamb vindaloo, banana fritters, samosas in mint sauce.

None of these crackerjack women are wearing
high heels or passionate perfume or carnal lipstick.
They gossip grouchily, mouths full of chickpea batter,
wiping devil-may-care hands upon whisker washed jeans.

The bank manager in a stock-tie brooch has been governing
the reverse end of the gossamer collapsible table all afternoon,
garishly coquetting a chirping twenty-year-old curvy Latina
clad in ripped overalls and a Candy Cane Tulip arm sleeve.

My mother's animated indigo eyes never brush their way,
immersed in her invigorating canvas and bottomless blushes,
now commanding a flawless symmetry of violet and celeste
for vivifying an Indian summer evening sky ballet.

Gamine

Arsenic-blue maidenhair
hammers at the French barn door
like homicidal harbinger banshees,
or werewolves whittled from Baily's Beads

Platinum pixies pamper the stargaze hothouse
birthing bullheaded bouquets of floss flowers,
quicksilver pomp trailing Lusty Gallant
and drunk-tank pink, the tender articulation
in a flame-of-burnt-brandy butterfly kiss

Often, I will summon scapegrace zigzag Jobyna:
unvarnished eventide of black-market milestones
ill-mannered flower moon nighthawk kiss-curls
wildcat moxie in labyrinthine lifeblood
hunting steeplechases in cerulean snowstorms

Monophonic, we watered waxen orchids
crooning gypsy jazz
for understory tea fields
graphed camisado shortcuts throughout
pine-floored Greek Revival plantations
branded tin lizzie go-carts
with dirt road donuts
lindy-hopped the cha-cha-cha
wielding origami legwork
cross-examined historic lavender hotels
hunting the revised ghost of Jesse James

divined japa mala jumble sales
from Americana roots-rock ash heaps

Between these discolored heartbeats
thrashing with tobacco shiraz and inanimate elegies,
you still lie in wait, a curtained gator
transporting twigs atop its pancaked skull,
luring in catbirds patchworking platform nests

Your koi pond essence lingers
like stolen apple perfume:

an atomic tootsie outlaw
in that rumpled peplum dress,
bumbling bungee cord sneaker boots,
catapulting rotting rogue branches
into tectonic missing lakes

Three Stickling Sisters

There was a time when three sphinxlike sisters
draped in heartless curtain bangs felt blessed by
the gods of Protestant piano, pulses synched like
smoked alligator watches, undetermined lips unkissed,
tamed with salmon satin, fledgling and tigerish.

The oldest sister, steeped in subtlety and bergamot,
folds like a fuchsia lace Fontage fan
within the cryptic entrails of my memory.
I recall the tapered half-moon of her heels
as she danced barefoot at a humanist wedding.
Her dress could have been Limerick lace or swanskin cloth
or tailored from strawberry moons;
it only ever existed to articulate her keynote.

The middle sister sketched throughout worship,
foxily skirting boiling philippic on lakes of lambs' blood,
saccharine wives weeping for homes of unhewn stones.
She penciled nautical Lolitas with overworked wings,
imperial bassett hounds storming rose white rabbits.
She once imparted a withering poppy to the acrylic tithe box,
underscoring it with an epiphany from Emily:
"Because I could not stop for Death..."

The youngest sister, all charismatic shoulders in eyelet,
got hitched to the very first doctor she could bushwhack
with her peridot artillery, ever the reckless rainmaker.
He spoon-fed her pivotal Prada, carbonated Chanel, defensive
Dior;

tutu skirts in Spanish pink, bootcut jeans against collapsible
backgrids;
opera pearls, abalone matinee beads, vignetted rings with ruby
halos;
a feathery iota of untamed Marie Antoinette teardrops
worn only to afternoon tea dances and green funerals.

Cemetery Birds

her conclusive marker is a cat's eye teardrop
armored with a revering Texas pearl Madonna
fenestral fiberglass Ladies of Fatima
shrouding the atrophied sweep
of hydrangea-high hillsides

sadness is a wall between two gardens

a finial French gold marble footstone
fringes a byzantine epitaph

peace perfect peace

bleeding hearts hemming
the burial axis contoured by
a pig iron picket grave rail

oblations of opalite owls
carnelian cranes
fossil coral finfoots
star garnet swallows

like the ripples, like the ripples in the stream

an emerald copper centerpiece
of Saint Abanoub
the child martyr
atomic hands plumed in prayer
engrosses rock doves fleeing cliffrose canyons

ageless beauty, running wild, pins it with a star

Sochraide

Mamò wore her Berlin Iron mourning shamrock brooch
to Daddy's second funeral, the one cluttered with
Clearwater cousins clad in composite turquoise,
blackened silver, beaded bone mermaids.

She sat stiff-backed atop the tobacco leaf pew,
her overclouded complexion wilting like
an iolite sky staggered by steam devils.

This time around, she resisted resounding
"Old Rugged Cross",
"Blessed Assurance",
"Because He Lives".

There were not enough chantries
in that tone-deaf church
to loosen the lamentation
from her heartless heartbreak,
the unseemly magdalens
from her secluded beadroll.

She absorbed my unquiet hand,
a distressed dove in hers,
the gritty gossamer gravity
of her moonstone cataracts
rooting my voiceless renegade.

"My *aingeal, a leanbh.*
He's scrubbing down those unswept stars.
You can always, always divine him in the dark."

Acknowledgment of Publications

Haikuniverse
May 2018
"Photo Album"

Free Lit Review
May 2018
"Absquatulate"

Gone Lawn
June 2018
"Prostrate"

Little Rose Magazine
June 2018
"Driving by An Oklahoma Wedding"

Niveous Magazine
June 2018
"Dogtrot"

Rabid Oak
June 2018
"Easter"
"No-Tell"

Black Dog Review
June 2018
"Cultivation"

SurVision Magazine
July 2018
"Upon Turning Thirty"

Dunes Review
July 2018
"Decibel"

riverbabble
July 2018
"Cemetery Birds"

Peeking Cat Poetry
October 2018
"Royal Botanical Gardens, Sydney"

Papercuts Magazine
Fall 2018
"No-Tell" (reprint)

Picaroon Poetry
January 2019
"The Blind Pig Live"

vox poetica
January 2019
"Dude Ranch Dues"

Soul-Lit
Spring 2019
"Sochraide"

Nebo Magazine
Fall Issue 2020
"Sochraide" (reprint)

The Creativity Webzine
January 2021
"Prostrate" (reprint)

The Stray Branch
Spring 2022
"No-Tell" (reprint)
"Cemetery Birds" (reprint)

Across the Margin
March 2022
"Reparations"
"A Bathing Beauty"
"Unpolishing Black Pearls"

Ginosko Literary Journal
Spring 2022
"Cemetery Birds" (reprint)
"Prostrate" (reprint)
"No-Tell" (reprint)
"Cultivation" (reprint)

The Disappointed Housewife
June 2022
"Painting Party at an Indian Buffet"

Book of Matches Literary Magazine
Summer 2022
"Sea Ledge"

Eunoia Review
July 2022
"Decibel" (reprint)
"Upon Turning Thirty" (reprint)

Brazos River Review
July 2022
"Obsequies"
"If Your Villain Returns"
"No Crystal Ball Needed"

The Wise Owl
Summer 2022
"Incoherence"
"Gamine"

ABOUT THE AUTHOR

Megan Denese Mealor is a wordsmith of all that is shattered, shuttered, unhinged, preposterous, and moonstruck. She has authored two full-length poetry collections: *Bipolar Lexicon* (Unsolicited Press, 2018) and *Blatherskite* (Clare Songbirds House Publishing, 2019). Her first poetry chapbook, *A Mourning Dove's Wishbone,* is a loose-fitting love story to the uncanny, the Daliesque, and the ghoulishly beautiful.

A two-time Pushcart Prize nominee, Megan's poetry, fiction, and photography have been featured worldwide in such laudable literary publications as *Digital Americana, Black Heart Magazine, Sick Lit Magazine, Hello Horror, A Long Story Short, Gone Lawn, The*

Furious Gazelle, Liquid Imagination, The Belleville Park Pages, The Bitchin' Kitsch, Deep South Magazine, The Scarlet Leaf Review, Across the Margin, Brazos River Review, and *Jersey Devil Press,* amongst many others. In 2018, she was selected as the Featured Poet of *Neologism Poetry Journal*'s November 2018 issue.

Megan is a proud mother to 8-year-old son Jesse, who was diagnosed with autism at age three. Megan acts as his in-home behavioral and speech therapist. Her many oddball hobbies include swimming, yoga, photography, painting, making jewelry boxes, baking, astrology, the study of spirituality, volunteering at an animal shelter and a food bank, collecting 1980s cartoons memorabilia, watching the goriest horror movies out there, studying female killers in preparation for writing a book, alligators and crocodiles, origami, scrapbooking, old-school board games, air hockey, crossword puzzles, breathing new life into thrift store furniture, and spending as much time as possible with her son at malls, playgrounds, water parks, alligator farms, beaches, and Walmart.

Despite a decades-long battle with bipolar disorder, Megan is only now beginning to respond to treatment and therapy. All her life, throughout the vicious anguish and staggering inner traumas which regularly affect those suffering from mental illness, writing has always remained Megan's most powerful, purifying outlet for unleashing those indefinable demons. For her, poetry is just the enigma needed to harmonize a jagged heart.

Megan haunts, prowls, and politely curtsies in her graffiti-hearted native land of Jacksonville, Florida. She and Tony, her husband of ten years, are happily raising their son Jesse, along with three mollycoddled rescue cats Trigger, Lulu, and Hobbes. The quilted little family resides in a cavernous, cozy townhouse ornamented with blue rose hurricane lamps, Bavarian Forest cuckoo clocks, and vintage ads for Victorian inventions.

You won't often find Megan on any man-made map, as she possesses a vexatious habit of running wild when the stars exhale just right.

www.ingramcontent.com/pod-product-compliance
Lightning Source LLC
Chambersburg PA
CBHW050025170726
48282CB00025B/558
* 9 7 8 9 3 9 5 2 2 4 0 1 7 *